What Are Wheels and Axles?

by Helen Frost

Consulting Editor: Gail Saunders-Smith, Ph.D.

Consultant: Philip W. Hammer, Ph.D.
Assistant Director of Education
American Institute of Physics

Pebble Books

an imprint of Capstone Press
Mankato, Minnesota

Pebble Books are published by Capstone Press
151 Good Counsel Drive, P.O. Box 669, Mankato, Minnesota 56002
http://www.capstone-press.com

Printed in the United States of America.

1 2 3 4 5 6 06 05 04 03 02 01

Library of Congress Cataloging-in-Publication Data
Frost, Helen, 1949–
What are wheels and axles? / by Helen Frost.
p. cm.—(Looking at simple machines)
Includes bibliographical references (p. 23) and index.
ISBN 0-7368-0850-7
1. Wheels—Juvenile literature. 2. Axles—Juvenile literature.
[1. Wheels. 2. Axles.] I.Title. II. Series.
TJ181.5. F76 2001
621.8′11—dc21

00-009869

Summary: Simple text and photographs present wheels and axles and their function as a simple machine.

Note to Parents and Teachers

The Looking at Simple Machines series supports national science standards for units on understanding work, force, and tools. This book describes wheels and axles and illustrates how they make work easier. The photographs support early readers in understanding the text. This book also introduces early readers to subject-specific vocabulary words, which are defined in the Words to Know section. Early readers may need assistance to read some words and to use the Table of Contents, Words to Know, Read More, Internet Sites, and Index/Word List sections of the book.

Table of Contents

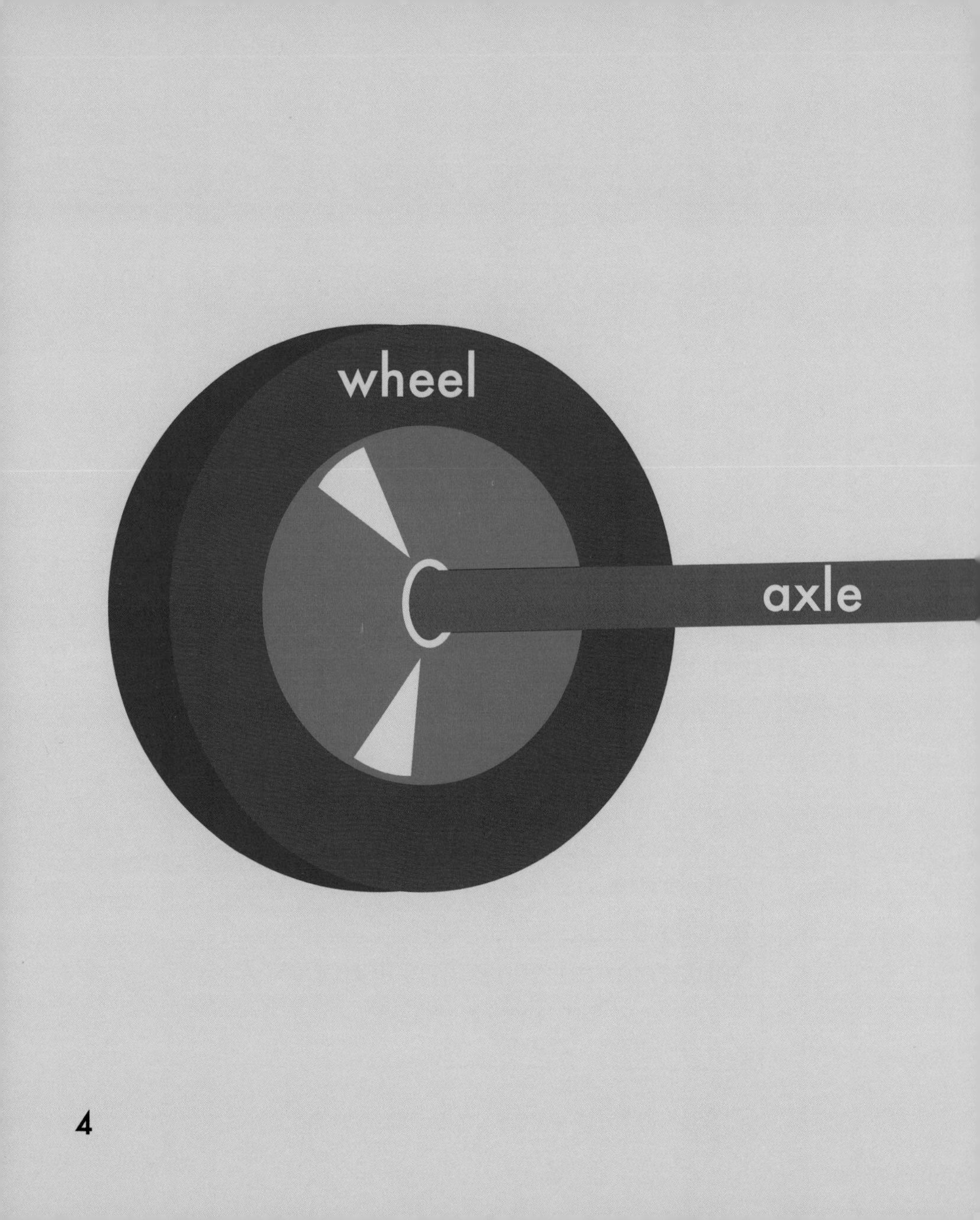
wheel
axle

A wheel and axle is
a simple machine.

A wheel is round.

axle

An axle is a rod
attached to a wheel.

axle

The axle goes through
the center of the wheel.

force

The wheel turns when
a force turns the axle.

force

The axle turns when
a force turns the wheel.

A fishing reel is
a wheel and axle.

A windmill is
a wheel and axle.

A doorknob is
a wheel and axle.

Words to Know

axle—a rod attached to the center of a wheel; the wheel and axle turn together; a small force on the wheel changes to a large force on the axle.

doorknob—a round handle that is turned to open a door; the knob is a kind of wheel; it is attached to an axle.

force—a push or a pull on an object; force makes objects start moving, speed up, change direction, or stop moving.

reel—a spool or wheel on which fishing line is wound

simple machine—a tool that makes work easier; work is using a force to move an object across a distance; a wheel and axle is an example of a simple machine.

wheel—a round object that turns on an axle; a wheel moves a greater distance than an axle; wheels are used to move objects.

windmill—a machine powered by the wind